The Wild West

LEVEL ONE   **400 HEADWORDS**

OXFORD

UNIVERSITY PRESS

Great Clarendon Street, Oxford OX2 6DP

Oxford University Press is a department of the University of Oxford. It furthers the University's objective of excellence in research, scholarship, and education by publishing worldwide in

Oxford New York

Auckland Cape Town Dar es Salaam Hong Kong Karachi Kuala Lumpur Madrid Melbourne Mexico City Nairobi New Delhi Shanghai Taipei Toronto

With offices in

Argentina Austria Brazil Chile Czech Republic France Greece Guatemala Hungary Italy Japan Poland Portugal Singapore South Korea Switzerland Thailand Turkey Ukraine Vietnam

OXFORD and OXFORD ENGLISH are registered trade marks of Oxford University Press in the UK and in certain other countries

© Oxford University Press 2010

The moral rights of the author have been asserted

Database right Oxford University Press (maker)

First published in Dominoes 2002

2018

12

ISBN: 978 0 19 424769 6 BOOK
ISBN: 978 0 19 463952 1 BOOK AND AUDIO PACK

No unauthorized photocopying

Printed in China

This book is printed on paper from certified and well-managed sources.

ACKNOWLEDGEMENTS

Illustrations by: Neil Gower p 2; Simon Gurr pp 49, 50; Mark Ward pp 6, 12, 13, 18, 19, 25, 30, 42, 44.

The publisher would like to thank the following for permission to reproduce photographs: Bridgeman Art Library Ltd pp 3 (Covered wagons heading west (oil on canvas), Wyeth, Newell Convers (1882-1945/Peter Newark American Pictures), 4 (Trapper/Peter Newark American Pictures), 9 (Sioux Indians hunting buffalo, 1835 (oil on canvas), Catlin, George (1794-1872)/Peter Newark American Pictures), 10, 48 & 51 (Sitting Bull, Sioux Chief, c.1885, Barry, David Frances (1854-1934), 11 & 51 (Battle of Little Bighorn, 25th June 1876 (oil on canvas), Paxson, Edgar Samuel (1852-1915)/Peter Newark American Pictures), 15 (Portrait of Allan Pinkerton, (20th century)/Peter Newark American Pictures), 15 (Pinkerton's National Detective Agency, *We Never Sleep* (litho), American School, (19th century)/Peter Newark American Pictures), 16 & 40 (Wyatt Earp (1848-1929)/Peter Newark American Pictures), 20 (*Wild Bill* American School, (19th century)/Peter Newark Western Americana), 21 (Front cover of *Wild Bill's Last Trail*, American School, (19th century)/Peter Newark American Pictures), 22 & 40 (*Frank and Jesse James* c.1870, American Photographer, (19th century)/Peter Newark American Pictures), 23 (*Frank and Jesse James gang robbery*/Peter Newark American Pictures), 25 & 26 (Billy the Kid, American School, (19th century) / Private Collection / Peter Newark American Pictures), 27 & 45 (Billy The Kid shoots a bartender, illustration from the *Police Gazette*, American School, (19th century)/Peter Newark Western Americana),32, 40 & 51 (Buffalo Bill Cody (1846-1917)/ Peter Newark American Pictures), 35, 46 & 51 (Poster advertising Buffalo Bill's Wild West Show (colour litho), American School, (19th century)/Peter Newark Western Americana), 36 & 40 (Nat Love, c.1870 (photo), (19th century)/Peter Newark American Pictures), 39 & 40 (Davy Crockett/Peter Newark American Pictures), 39, 40 & 51 (Geronimo, American School, (20th century)/Peter Newark American Pictures), 39 (Bella Starr, 1889 (colour litho), American School, (19th century)/Peter Newark American Pictures), 41 (Bella Starr, 1889 (colour litho), American School, (19th century)/Peter Newark American Pictures); Corbis pp 5 (Kit Carson/Bettman), 14 (The Eagles Dressed as Cowboys/Henry Diltz), 25 (Butch Cassidy/ Jonathan Blair), 32 (Buffalo Bill's Traveling Troupe), 39 (Charles Marion Russell/Lake County Museum); Getty Images pp 1 (The Mittens/James Randklev/Stone), 37 (Cowboy and horse at dusk/Gary Holscher/Stone); Kobal Collection pp 0 (*Maverick*/Icon Productions/Cooper, Andrew), 0 (*Unforgiven*/Warner Bros), 28 (*Butch Cassidy and the Sundance Kid*); Mary Evans Picture Library pp 33 (Colonel William Frederick Cody/Explorer Archives), 34 & 40 (Annie Oakley); Ronald Grant Archive pp 0 (*Wyatt Earp*), 0 (*Dances with Wolves*), 0 (*Dances with Wolves*), 0 (Will Smith in *Wild Wild West*), 0 (*Geronimo*), 0 (*The Quick and the Dead*), 17 & 47 (Gunfight at the OK Corral), 29 (*Butch Cassidy and the Sundance Kid*).

Cover: Getty Images (Sioux/Roger Viollet).

DOMINOES

Series Editors: Bill Bowler and Sue Parminter

The Wild West

John Escott

John Escott has written many books for readers of all ages, and particularly enjoys writing crime and mystery thrillers. He was born in the west of England, but now lives on the south coast. When he is not writing, he visits second-hand bookshops, watches videos of old Hollywood movies, and takes long walks along empty beaches. He has also written *The Wild West, A Pretty Face, Kidnap!* and *The Big Story*, and retold *William Tell and Other Stories* for Dominoes.

OXFORD
UNIVERSITY PRESS

BEFORE READING

1 Look at these pictures from films. Which three show the Wild West best?
Tick the boxes.

a □   b □   c □

d □   e □   f □

g □   h □

2 Complete this sentence. Use a dictionary to help you.

When I see the words 'Wild West' I think of . . .

'GO WEST, YOUNG MAN!'

'Go West, young man!' said an American **newspaper** in 1850. And thousands of Americans went.

But people started moving to the American West nearly fifty years earlier. In 1803, American **president** Thomas Jefferson, **bought** thousands of kilometres of land from the French for fifteen million dollars. The land was west of the Mississippi River and east of the Rocky Mountains. (In today's United States you can find Nebraska, Iowa, Kansas, **Missouri**, Oklahoma, **Arkansas**, and **Louisiana** there.)

The next year, Jefferson asked two men to go through this land to the Pacific. 'When you find flowers and trees by the road, look carefully at them and write about them,' Jefferson said. 'And talk to the people, too.' These two men were Meriwether Lewis and William Clark. In May 1804, Lewis and Clark went west with forty-six men. It was November 1805 when they arrived at the Pacific.

These were the early years of the '**Wild** West'. A time when the names Kit Carson, Sitting Bull, **Wyatt Earp**, Wild Bill Hickok, Butch Cassidy, Annie Oakley, and many more, **became** famous across America.

newspaper people read about things that happen every day in this

president the most important person in a country

buy (*past* **bought**) to give money for something

Missouri /mɪˈzʊəri/

Arkansas /ˈɑː(r)kənsɑː/

Louisiana /luːˌiːziˈænə/

wild interesting and exciting

Wyatt Earp /ˈwaɪət ɜː(r)p/

become (*past* **became**) to begin to be

1

Western Trails

There were three important **trails** to the West, and they all began near the town of Saint Louis.

In 1821, the first white man left to **travel** the 1,300 kilometres to **Santa Fe** in New Mexico. Soon, this became an important trail to the Southwest. Between 1826 and 1835, 1,500 men and 750 **wagons** travelled along the Santa Fe Trail, carrying shirts and trousers, knives and many more things to **sell** to the people of New Mexico.

At the end of the 1830s, it was not easy to find work in the East, and people did not have much money. They read about the West in books and newspapers and said, 'Everything is better there. Let's go West!'

Early in the 1840s, thousands of families left their homes and travelled 3,200 kilometres to California and Oregon. It took them about six months.

The Oregon and California Trails became the two most famous trails. For the first 1,900 kilometres, the trails went across Kansas, along by the River **Platte**, and through the south of the Rocky **Mountains**. After that, the Oregon

trail a road across wild country

travel to go

Santa Fe /ˌsæntə ˈfeɪ/

wagon a kind of car with horses

sell (*past* **sold**) to take money for something

Platte /plæt/

mountains very big hills

Trail went north to Oregon City. From there it was not far to the Pacific. The California Trail went south to Sacramento.

Families travelled along the trails in wagons or on horses. Some walked. Many became ill and died before they got near the West. **Indians** (now called **Native Americans**) killed some of them.

From 1841 to the 1880s, about 350,000 people travelled to the West by these trails. Then the **railroads** came, and most families didn't need the trails. 'Now we can travel by train,' they said.

Wagon Trains

Many families going West went with a wagon train. The 'train' was a number of wagons travelling together. Sometimes there were a hundred wagons carrying two or three hundred people. Horses pulled the wagons and they went about twenty-five kilometres a day.

The first wagons were very large wagons from France. Later, families travelled in smaller wagons.

Indians/Native Americans they lived in North America before white people

railroad a train travels on this

3

A mountain man

Mountain Men

The 1830s and 1840s were the years of the 'mountain men'. They lived in the mountains, killed animals there, and sold the **skins** to make money. Sometimes they took people through the mountains. They knew the best trails, and were often good friends with the Indians.

Kit Carson

One of the most famous mountain men was Kit Carson. When he was seventeen, he left his home in Missouri and **joined** a wagon train going to Santa Fe. From there he travelled north. When he was nineteen he went to kill animals in California. It was the first of many visits to the mountains of the West.

In January 1833, Carson was with about fifty mountain men on the Arkansas River in Colorado. Some Indians took nine of their horses. The next day, Kit, with twelve more men, travelled more than sixty kilometres to find, **fight**, and kill those Indians.

But he was usually a good friend of Native Americans. His first wife was an Arapaho Indian, and his second wife was a woman from the **Cheyenne tribe**. He had a daughter, and in 1842 he took her to Missouri because he wanted her to go to school there. On the road to Missouri, he met a man called John C. Fremont.

skin the outside of an animal's body

join to go with

fight (*past* **fought**) to hit someone again and again

Cheyenne /ʃaɪˈæn/

tribe a big family of Indians

Fremont worked for the American **government**, finding new trails across the West. Carson knew the land well and for the next five years he helped Fremont with his work. These years made Kit Carson famous.

Later, he worked with the American **army**. He was an army **scout** in the **war** with the **Navajo** Indians. The Navajos fought with many different tribes of

Kit Carson

Indians in the West. In 1864, some of these tribes joined the 'white man's' army to fight the Navajos. After the Navajos lost the war, and their land, 8,000 Navajo men, women and children went on 'The Long Walk' – 480 kilometres from Arizona to New Mexico.

Kit Carson was fifty-nine when he died in 1868. He never learned to read.

The Pony Express

At first, getting letters from the East to the West of America was slow. Then, in 1860, came the **Pony Express**. Its horses and **riders** were fast.

They travelled from St Joseph in Missouri to Sacramento in California. Every rider travelled 120 kilometres before giving his bag of letters to the next rider. The 3,120 kilometres from St Joseph to Sacramento took twenty-six riders ten days in all.

government the people who work with the president

army a large number of people who fight for their country

scout a person who knows the land well and goes in front of an army

war fighting between countries or tribes

Navajo /ˈnævəˌhəʊ/

pony a small horse

express very fast

rider a person who goes on a horse

READING CHECK

Are these sentences true or false? Tick the boxes.

		True	False
a	American people started to go west in 1850.	☐	☑
b	The French sold a lot of land to Thomas Jefferson in 1803.	☐	☐
c	Lewis and Clark went through this land to the Pacific.	☐	☐
d	The Santa Fe trail went to the north-east.	☐	☐
e	People travelled west in wagons and later on trains.	☐	☐
f	Kit Carson worked for the American government and in the army.	☐	☐
g	The Pony Express took twenty-six days to go from St Joseph to Sacramento.	☐	☐

WORD WORK

1 Look at the pictures and write the missing words. They all come from Chapter 1.

When we went west we didn't take the  (a) *railroad*

My mother and father travelled by  (b)................ . I rode

on my little  (c)................ . One day we saw an

(d)................ . Then we went across the  (e)................

2 Use the letters to make words from Chapter 1. Then write the sentences.

a In 1775 A$_c^m {}_r^a {}_e^i$ wanted to be free from the British g$^{m\,n\,t\,v\,e}_{\ \ n\,r\,e\,o}$.

In 1775 America wanted to be free from the
British government.

b Do you want to b^y_u a n$^{p\,r\,w\,e}_{p\,s\,a\,e}$? That shop s$^l_l{}^s_e$ them.

c Lincoln b$^{c\,a}_{m\,e}{}^e$ the American p$^{d\,r\,t}_{n\,s\,e}{}^e_i$ in 1860.

d People bought w$^d_l{}^i$ animal s$^k_n{}^s_i$ from Kit Carson.

e Our s$^c_t{}^o_u$ found new t$^l_r{}^s_a{}^i$ across the l$^d_n{}^a$.

f I wouldn't like to j$^n_i{}^o$ the a$^m_r{}^y$ and f$^g_h{}^t_i$ in a w^r_a.

g Those Indian r$^{d\,s}_{r\,e}{}^i$ are from the Arapaho t$^b_r{}^e_i$.

h It's nice to t$^l_r{}^v_a{}^e$ on an e$^p_r{}^s_s{}^x_e$ train.

GUESS WHAT

The next chapter is about Native Americans and White people. Are these sentences about NA (Native Americans) or WP (White people)? Tick the boxes.

		NA	WP
a	Rivers, trees, and mountains were living things for them.	☐	☐
b	They liked to buy and sell land.	☐	☐
c	They lost 700 million square kilometres of land between 1853 and 1874.	☐	☐
d	They only killed animals when they needed to eat.	☐	☐
e	They wanted to become rich.	☐	☐
f	They wanted to buy the Black Hills of Dakota.	☐	☐

7

NATIVE AMERICANS

Native Americans – or 'Red Indians' – lived in North America for thousands of years before the people from Europe arrived. There were many different tribes, most with different languages. Tribes had their lands for **hunting**, and sometimes they fought about them. But the land, the mountains, the rivers, and the trees were living things for them. The Indians understood the land. They took from it only the things they needed to live.

But to the 'white man', land was something to buy and sell and to make money with. White men wanted to get land for their **farms** and **mines**.

The United States government did not understand the Native Americans' love of the land – its mountains and rivers. They asked Indians to give some of their lands to white men, and at first they did. But then the white men wanted more and more land, and the government moved the Indians into **reservations**.

Between 1853 and 1874, the Indians lost 700 million square kilometres of land to the white men.

hunt to find and kill a wild animal for its meat or skin

farm a house with land in the country

mine people get things from under the land here

reservation land that white men didn't want and gave to the Indians

8

The Buffalo

The Native Americans hunted and killed only the animals they needed, and no more. For many tribes, the most important animal of all was the **buffalo**. They ate buffalo meat, and buffalo skin became trousers, dresses and shoes for them to wear, and homes for them to live in.

Hunting buffalo

When the Native Americans saw white men hunting and killing thousands of buffaloes, they were afraid and angry. Some wanted to fight with the white men.

Sitting Bull

The most famous Indian of all was **Chief** Sitting Bull, a **Sioux** Indian born in South Dakota in about 1831. He was the Sioux tribe's most famous chief.

Sitting Bull did not like the white man. In 1863 **soldiers attacked** some of his men when they went hunting. For the next two years, an angry Sitting Bull fought with the US Army. In 1864 he took his men to fight two thousand American soldiers in the **Battle** of Kildeer Mountain.

In 1868, some Sioux Indians moved to a big reservation in the Black Hills of Dakota. But, in 1874, somebody found **gold** in the Black Hills, and white men quickly moved into the hills to begin looking for more. The Indians fought them, and the army could not stop the fighting.

buffalo a big North American animal

chief the most important man in a tribe

Sioux /suː/

soldier a person in an army

attack to start fighting

battle when two armies fight

gold an expensive yellow metal

Sitting Bull

In 1875, the US government asked the Sioux chiefs to meet them. They wanted to buy the Black Hills from the Indians and to put gold mines there. Sitting Bull did not go to meet the government people, but he sent them a **message**. 'We do not want white men here. The Black Hills are our hills. We are ready to fight the white men for them.'

In June, 1876, Sitting Bull sent a message to all the Sioux, Arapaho and Cheyenne tribes. 'We must fight the white man!' And 10,000 Indians got ready.

Some days later, 1,000 of them fought 1,300 white soldiers in Montana. The fighting went on for six hours. When it finished and the Indians at last went away, there were only nine dead white soldiers.

All the Sioux Indians then moved on to the Little Big Horn River. A week later, George Custer and his soldiers found them there.

The Indians knew Custer well. Eight years before, in 1868, Custer and his soldiers killed over a hundred sleeping Indians – most of them women, children and old people – when he attacked a Cheyenne village near the Washita River. He also fought the Sioux in the Black Hills and helped to bring the gold miners there. When Custer arrived at Little Big Horn, the Sioux remembered these things and were angry.

message
information that
one person gives
to another

The Battle of the Little Big Horn, on June 25, 1876, was the most famous of all Indian battles. In an hour, about 3,000 Native Americans killed Custer and his 250 soldiers. When people in the East read the story of the Little Big Horn battle in their newspapers many were very angry with the Indians for killing Custer.

After the battle, Sitting Bull took his people into Canada, but in 1881 he brought them home again. By then, the US government had the Black Hills and there was nothing Sitting Bull could do about it.

Later, Sitting Bull travelled to many cities in America and Canada with Buffalo Bill Cody and his Wild West **Show**. Buffalo Bill liked the Indian chief and gave him a beautiful horse to take with him when he left the show. After that, Sitting Bull went home to live quietly for some years.

At about that time some of the Indians began to say 'Our dead men are coming back, and the white man is going to leave our land'. The army did not like this. In 1890, they tried to stop these new Indian **beliefs** by killing about 200 Sioux men, women and children in a battle in South Dakota.

Sitting Bull did nothing to stop the new beliefs in his tribe. On December 14, 1890, **police officers** went to get him. There was a fight, and Sitting Bull died in it.

show something that you watch

belief something that people think is true

police officer a policeman or policewoman

The Battle of the Little Big Horn

READING CHECK

Choose the right words to finish the sentences.

a Native American tribes spoke . . .
1 one language. ☐
2 different languages. ☑
3 English. ☐

b The US government asked . . .
1 Indians to give land to white people. ☐
2 white people to give land to Indians. ☐
3 white people to live near Indians. ☐

c Indians killed buffaloes . . .
1 to stop white people getting them. ☐
2 because they liked killing. ☐
3 for their skin and meat. ☐

d Sitting Bull was from the . . .
1 Cheyenne tribe. ☐
2 Arapaho tribe. ☐
3 Sioux tribe. ☐

e He wanted . . .
1 no white men or gold mines in the Black Hills. ☐
2 to kill all white men. ☐
3 to sell the Black Hills to the US government. ☐

f The Indians killed Custer at Little Big Horn because . . .
1 they didn't like any white men. ☐
2 Custer did many bad things to the Indians. ☐
3 they were bad and he was good. ☐

g Sitting Bull died in . . .
1 a fight with some policemen. ☐
2 an accident in Buffalo Bill's Wild West Show. ☐
3 a battle with the US army. ☐

WORD WORK

1 Complete the puzzles with Indian names from Chapter 2.

a Name the chief. ....

b Name the battle. ....

2 Use the words in the Indian head-dress to complete the sentences.

a ...Police officers... killed Sitting Bull.

b Indians were free to move about the land before they went to live in ....

c Once thousands of .... lived wild in North America.

d Sitting Bull was a famous Indian ....

e White people found .... in the Black Hills of Dakota.

f Indian men learnt to .... animals when they were young boys.

g People build .... to get gold from the land.

h Custer died in the .... of the Little Big Horn.

i .... usually fight with guns.

j In the past Indians sometimes .... wagon trains.

k Indians sent smoke .... across many kilometres.

l People in the east of America liked seeing Wild West ....

(words in head-dress: attacked, battle, buffaloes, chief, gold, messages, hunt, mines, police officers, shows, reservations, soldiers)

GUESS WHAT

The next chapter is about good men and bad men.
What are you going to read about? Tick the boxes.

	Yes	No
a There were detective offices in the Wild West.	☐	☐
b These offices were never far when people needed them.	☐	☐
c There were often fights between men in Wild West towns.	☐	☐
d In the Wild West good men and bad men were usually not very different.	☐	☐
e Hollywood films always tell the true story of what happened in the Wild West.	☐	☐

THE LAW OF THE GUN

crime killing someone or taking money from someone

law the rule that says what people must or must not do

Abilene
/ˌæbəˈliːn/

cowboy a man who looks after cows

gun a person can fight with this

gamble to play games for money

When the first people moved from towns in the East to the West, there was a lot of **crime**. Later, when at last the **law** arrived in the West, the law offices and lawmen were often eighty kilometres or more away. So people often had to fight crime without the help of the law.

Abilene and Dodge City were two towns famous for crime. **Cowboys** came here with their **guns** and their money after weeks on the trail. They drank and **gambled** and some men died in fights.

There was crime in the towns near gold mines, too, and people in the East began to call the West the 'Wild West'. And it was wild.

The Pinkertons

Allan Pinkerton came from Scotland to Chicago in 1842, and started Pinkerton's Detectives.

'We never sleep', it said on the front window of every Pinkerton's office. This and their picture of an open eye got them the name 'Eyes'. And this later gave the name 'private eye' to any detective not working for the police.

Allan Pinkerton

The Pinkertons became famous in 1861. In that year Allan Pinkerton learned that some men wanted to kill President Abraham Lincoln, and he stopped them.

The Pinkerton Eye

15

Wyatt Earp

One of the West's most famous lawmen was Wyatt Earp. He was born in **Illinois**, and had four brothers – Virgil, Morgan, James and Warren. When Wyatt was sixteen years old, his family moved to California. He worked on the railroad, and he was a buffalo hunter and a **stagecoach** driver. Then Wyatt went to Wichita and became a city police officer there. His brother James lived in Wichita.

In 1876, Wyatt moved to Dodge City, Kansas, and was a police officer there for two years. In that time, he met the famous Wild West gunman Doc Holliday.

Illinois /ˌɪləˈnɔɪ/

stagecoach a kind of bus with horses

deputy a person who helps someone

sheriff a person who looks after the law in a town in the USA

US marshal the head of the police in a city in the USA

In 1878, Earp left Dodge City and travelled to New Mexico and California. Then in 1879 he went to live in the wild Arizona town of Tombstone, famous for its gold mines – and for crime. Soon after, Doc Holliday, and Wyatt's two brothers Morgan and Warren arrived in the town. In July 1880, Wyatt became **deputy sheriff**. His brother Virgil was a deputy **US marshal**.

Then, in 1881, a big fight made the Earp brothers famous across the West.

Wyatt Earp

The famous gunfight at the OK **Corral** happened on October 26, 1881. The fight was between the Earp brothers and a **gang** of **criminals** called the Clanton Gang.

On the afternoon of October 26, Wyatt, Virgil and Morgan Earp, and Doc Holliday killed three of the Clanton Gang at the OK Corral. Virgil was the first to **shoot**. He killed one man. Doc shot and killed a second man, and Wyatt and Morgan shot and killed a third. Two men got away.

In the gunfight, the Clanton Gang shot Morgan, Virgil and Doc but they did not die. They didn't hit Wyatt at all.

The shooting took half a minute.

In the film *Gunfight at the OK Corral*, Wyatt, his brothers and Doc Holliday are good men fighting for the law. But today, some people say the gunfight was a fight between two gangs of criminals.

corral cowboys put cows in this to stop them running away

gang a number of people who work on a crime

criminal a person who does something that is against the law

shoot (*past* **shot**) to fight with a gun

Gunfight at the OK Corral

READING CHECK

Correct the mistakes in these sentences.

a Allan Pinkerton started Pinkerton's Detectives in ~~1824~~. *1842*

b He came to America from Ireland.

c It said 'We never close' on every Pinkerton's Detective office.

d Pinkerton's Detectives didn't stop a man from killing President Lincoln in 1861.

e Wyatt Earp had five brothers.

f Wyatt Earp worked as a gold miner in Wichita, and Dodge City.

g Wyatt Earp, two of his brothers, and Doc Holliday killed three men on September 26, 1881.

WORD WORK

1 These words don't match the pictures. Correct them.

a ~~gamble~~ *stagecoach*

b corral
....

d stagecoach
....

c lawmen
....

e cowboy
....

f gun
....

2 **Find words in the cowboy's tombstone to complete the sentences.**

JOHN LAW
1850-1895
Deputy Sheriff
and
deputy marshal

He fought crime
and criminals
and shot dead
all six men
in the Clanton brothers'
gang

a Killing someone is a ..crime.. .

b The Daltons were a ....
   of ....

c Wyatt Earp was a ....

d He .... at me,
   but he didn't hit me.

e Virgil Earp was a ....

f You mustn't break the ....!

GUESS WHAT

The next chapter is about another Wild West lawman and a criminal gang. What are you going to read about? Tick the boxes.

	Yes	No
a A fight in a Pony Express office.	☐	☐
b A man shooting a sheriff in the back of the head.	☐	☐
c A sheriff making his horse the deputy sheriff.	☐	☐
d Criminals taking money from a train.	☐	☐
e A criminal shooting a detective.	☐	☐
f A detective dying after drinking a cup of coffee.	☐	☐
g Detectives killing a nine-year-old boy.	☐	☐

LAWMEN AND GUNMEN 4

Wild Bill Hickok

James Butler Hickok was one of the West's most famous gunfighters. He always carried two guns, and could shoot well with his left or his right hand.

After his father died, James took his father's name, Bill. It became 'Wild Bill' after he was in a fight with a number of men in 1861. Hickok got work with the Pony Express in one of their offices in Nebraska. A **manager** and a third man worked with him.

On a July day in 1861, a man called Dave **McCanles** came to the Pony Express office with two friends. McCanles spoke to the Pony Express manager and got angry with him. A fight started. In the fight Hickok and the two Pony Express men shot McCanles and his friends dead.

Four years later a writer wrote about the shooting and about 'Wild Bill'. Not many of the things he wrote were true, but people loved reading them and the book sold well. More stories about 'Wild Bill' appeared later and Hickok was always called Wild Bill after that.

manager the most important person in an office

McCanles /məˈkænləs/

Wild Bill Hickok

Wild Bill joined the army and was an army scout for a time. On July 21, 1865, he shot and killed a gambler, Dave Tutt, in the street in Springfield, Missouri. Hickok was a gambler, too, and he didn't like Tutt. When he was about seventy metres away, Hickok shouted, 'Don't come any nearer, Tutt!' But Tutt took out his gun and began shooting. He didn't hit Hickok, but Hickok killed Tutt with one shot.

A 'Wild Bill' story

In August 1869, Hickok became sheriff of Ellis County, Kansas. He killed two men there, and then a month later became marshal at Hays City, Kansas.

In 1871, he moved to Abilene to become marshal there. Hickok kept the law with his guns and his knife. After leaving Abilene, he worked with Buffalo Bill's Wild West Show for a short time.

On August 2, 1876, a man came into a **saloon** in Deadwood City, South Dakota. He shot Hickok in the back of the head and killed him.

saloon a place where cowboys went to drink

Frank and Jesse James

In February, 1866, a gang of twelve riders arrived at the front door of a **bank** in Liberty, Missouri. They took $57,000 from the building and killed a young man in the street when they rode out of town. It was the first daytime bank **robbery** in America. Frank James was the **leader** of the gang. Soon after this, Frank's brother **Jesse** joined the gang. Jesse was the younger of the two brothers, but he soon became the leader.

Frank and Jesse James were the first criminals in America to **rob** banks *and* trains. In the American **Civil War** the brothers fought for the South – killing, and robbing banks and trains in the North. After the war they worked on the family farm for a short time. But between 1866 and 1882, the gang robbed seven trains, twelve banks and five stagecoaches.

In 1873 the gang robbed a train in Iowa. They pulled up the railroad and the train **crashed**. The driver died. The gang took all the bank money from the train, then went on to rob the people on the train.

bank people put money and expensive things here

robbery when criminals take money

leader the most important person

Jesse /'ʤesi/

rob to take something that is not yours from a place

civil war a war between two armies from one country

crash to hit something and stop suddenly

Frank and Jesse James

In 1874 a Pinkertons' detective went after the criminals, but Jesse shot him. After this, the Pinkertons wanted to get Jesse for killing their detective.

Frank and Jesse sometimes went back to the old family farm. The Pinkerton detectives heard about this. On a January night in 1875, some Pinkerton men went to the James's family farm. They threw a **bomb** in through a farmhouse window. Frank and Jesse were not there, but the bomb killed their nine-year-old brother – and their mother lost her hand.

Frank and Jesse went on robbing banks and trains for seven more years. But on April 3, 1882, one of the gang shot and killed Jesse. Some months later, Frank walked into a lawman's office and **surrendered**. He died at the age of seventy-two on February 18, 1915.

The James gang rob a train

bomb a thing that explodes noisily and can kill people

surrender to stop fighting because you cannot win

ACTIVITIES

READING CHECK

1 Correct eight more mistakes in the story of Bill Hickok.

             shoot

Bill Hickok could ~~write~~ well with his left or right hand. He and two Pony Express men

killed ten men in 1861. Four weeks later a writer put the story of 'Wild Bill' and the

shooting in a book. It was all true, but people didn't like reading it. Wild Bill Hickok

later became an army officer. He shot and killed Dave Tutt, a banker, in the street in

Springfield, Missouri. He worked with Buffalo Bill's Show for a long time. In 1876 a man

went to the saloon and shot Hickok in the front of the head.

2 Choose the correct words to complete the sentences about the James brothers.

a Frank was (older) / younger than Jesse.

b Jesse was gang leader before / after Frank.

c The James brothers took money from banks and trains / hotels.

d Frank / Jesse shot a Pinkerton's detective.

e Pinkerton detectives killed Jesse's younger sister / brother.

f Jesse's mother lost a foot / hand in the Pinkerton detectives' attack.

g One of the James gang killed Jesse / Frank in 1882.

h Frank died when he was twenty-seven / seventy-two.

WORD WORK

Use the words on the bottles to complete the sentences.

a All my money is in the
   bank .

b My uncle is the
   .... of a hotel.

c The Spanish .... began in 1936 and finished in 1939.

d In the Wild West people drank in ....

e The South of the USA .... to the North in 1865.

f Before the James brothers, American bank .... happened at night.

g He was the .... of a gang of criminals.

h The train .... into a tree.

i The James brothers .... stagecoaches too.

j The detectives threw a .... through the farmhouse window.

GUESS WHAT

**Here are two of the people in the next chapter.
Tick the boxes.**

Who . . .	Billy	Butch
a . . . worked on farms?		
b . . . took money from banks and trains?		
c . . . took horses and cows from people's farms?		
d . . . became very famous because of a film?		
e . . . first killed a man at the age of seventeen?		
f . . . visited New Mexico?		
g . . . worked in a butcher's shop?		

BUTCH AND THE KIDS

Billy the Kid

Billy the **Kid** was born with the name Henry McCarty in New York City on November 23, 1859. He was one of the most famous criminals of the American West.

After Henry's father died, his mother took him and his brother to Indiana. There she met (and later married) William Antrim and Henry changed his name to 'Billy Antrim'. The family moved to Wichita, then to Santa Fe, and then to Silver City in New Mexico. Henry's mother died there in 1874.

Billy the Kid

Henry was now called Kid Antrim. He was sixteen when he went to **jail** for the first time. But he got out and ran away from the town. In Arizona he became a cowboy for a time on a big farm. Then he began a life of crime again.

The Kid shot and killed his first man, after a fight in a saloon on August 17, 1877. Now Billy was a killer, and the lawmen were after him.

The Kid got out of Arizona quickly. He went to New Mexico and people there called him Billy Bonney. In New Mexico he joined a gang of criminals, taking cows and horses from people's farms. After the leader of this gang went to jail, Billy found work with a farmer – John Tunstall.

One day Sheriff William Brady killed Tunstall in a fight. Billy and a gang of his friends found and shot Brady on April 1, 1878. Not long after this, the Kid and ten gunmen stayed in a friend's house. The sheriff's men arrived and began shooting, but the Kid got away.

kid a young child

jail a place where people must stay when they do something wrong

*The Kid shoots
his first man*

On the night of December 19, 1880, Sheriff Pat Garrett found Billy and he went to jail, but he got out soon after and ran away, killing two men.

On July 14, 1881, Pat Garrett and two deputies went to the home of one of Billy's friends. It was dark when Billy arrived later. Garrett was there in the dark in one of the rooms. Billy looked in and asked, 'Who's there?' It was his last question. Garret shot and killed him dead there and then.

Billy was twenty-one years old when he died. Some say he killed twenty-one men – one for every year of his young life.

Butch Cassidy and the Sundance Kid

These two Wild West bank robbers are very famous today because of the film *Butch Cassidy and the Sundance Kid* (1969), with Paul Newman and Robert Redford.

Robert LeRoy Parker got the name 'Cassidy' from an old criminal called Mike Cassidy. Mike Cassidy gave Parker a gun when he was young and taught him to shoot.

After he left home, Parker worked on farms and, for a time, in a **butcher's** shop. From this he got the name 'Butch'. So now he was Butch Cassidy.

Then Butch began taking cows and horses from people's farms, and he went to jail for this for two years, from 1894 to 1896. When he came out, he and two more men robbed a bank in Idaho. They got away with $7,000. Soon Cassidy became the leader of a gang of criminals. One of the gang was Harry **Longabaugh** – the Sundance Kid.

When Longabaugh was seventeen he went to jail for **stealing** horses, but he got out and rode to Wyoming. Many criminals went there in those days to get away from the law.

For the next two or three years Sundance stole horses in Montana and Canada. And he met a woman called Etta Place. She soon became his lover. Then he joined Butch Cassidy's gang.

Butch and his gang robbed banks and trains. One of their biggest crimes was on June 2, 1899, when the gang robbed a train of $30,000. Soon after this, the railroads asked the

butcher's you can buy meat here

Longabaugh /ˈlɒŋɡəˌbɑː/

steal (*past* **stole**) to take something without asking

Pinkerton Detectives to hunt for Cassidy and his gang.

Butch, Sundance, and Etta Place went to South America. They bought a farm in Argentina, and for two or three years they lived without robbing banks and trains. But then Butch and Sundance started to rob again.

Etta Place went back to the USA, and the Pinkerton detectives began to look for the two criminals in South America. On November 3, 1908, Butch and Sundance robbed a Bolivian mine office. Three days later, soldiers came after them and found them in a small Bolivian village. There was a gunfight.

What happened next? Did Butch and Sundance die? Or did they escape back to the USA and live there with different names? Nobody knows.

The big train robbery from Butch Cassidy and the Sundance Kid

READING CHECK

Tick the correct names.

	Billy	Butch	Sundance
a He was born in New York City.	✔		
b He worked selling meat.			
c He first went to jail when he was sixteen.			
d He first went to jail when he was seventeen.			
e He shot Sheriff Brady.			
f He took money from a bank in Idaho.			
g He met his lover in Montana.			
h They say he killed twenty-one men.			
i Pat Garrett shot him dead.			
j They bought a farm in Argentina.			

WORD WORK

Use the words from the jail wall to complete the sentences.

a Robert Cassidy was a _butcher_ for a time.

b In 1883 they .... a woman called Bella Starr for taking a horse without paying for it.

c Have you got any .... horses on your land?

d .... sell meat.

e Criminals in the USA go to ....

f Butch and Sundance went to jail for .... horses.

g He was a .... of fifteen when his mother died.

h A .... puts criminals in jail to stop them getting away. He brings them things to eat and drink, too.

i When a killer kills people quickly and coldly, we can say he is '......................' them.

j When you say something is not true, perhaps to make people laugh, you are '......................'.

GUESS WHAT

**The next chapter is about Wild West shows and showmen.
Tick your answers. (Sometimes more than one answer is correct.)**

a How did Buffalo Bill get his name?

   1 Because he looked like a buffalo. ☐

   2 Because he came from the town of Buffalo. ☐

   3 Because he shot lots of buffalo. ☐

b Who worked in Buffalo Bill's Wild West Show?

   1 Chief Sitting Bull. ☐

   2 Wild Bill Hickok. ☐

   3 Jesse James. ☐

c What was Annie Oakley famous for?

   1 Her singing. ☐

   2 Her shooting. ☐

   3 Her beautiful face and hair. ☐

d What was different about Nat Love?

   1 He was a Chinese American cowboy. ☐

   2 He was a Mexican cowboy. ☐

   3 He was a black cowboy. ☐

WILD WEST SHOWS AND SHOOTING COMPETITIONS

Buffalo Bill Cody

Buffalo Bill was born William Frederick Cody in Iowa, in 1846. His father was a stagecoach driver. Later, Cody lived in Kansas and here the Kickapoo Indians taught him to ride a horse and to shoot a gun. When he was fifteen, Cody became a Pony Express rider in Wyoming. He once rode 618 kilometres without a stop – more than any rider before him.

He got the name 'Buffalo Bill' when he began to hunt and kill buffaloes for the railroads. The men building the railroads ate the buffaloes he shot, and the railroads gave him $500 a month for his work. He worked for them for eighteen months and killed about 4,280 buffaloes in this time.

A 'Buffalo Bill' book

In July 1868, Buffalo Bill Cody became a scout for the US Army in the Indian wars. He once rode 560 kilometres through the wildest Indian country in sixty hours.

Then Cody met Ned Buntline, a writer. Buntline wrote for the newspapers, and he also wrote books. He talked to Cody, and then went home to write about him. Soon after this, Buffalo Bill's name became famous across America. In 1872, Cody travelled to Chicago to be Buffalo Bill in one of Buntline's **plays** about Wild West scouts.

In 1876 Cody went back to the West to fight Indians with the army. After leaving the army, Cody started Buffalo Bill's Wild West Show, with a number of cowboys and Indians to help him.

The show began in **Omaha** in 1883. For the next twenty-five years it travelled across the USA and went to Europe. In the show people saw a **competition** for the fastest Pony Express rider, Indians attacking Custer at Little Big Horn, criminals robbing a stagecoach, a buffalo hunt, and Indians attacking a wagon train.

Buffalo Bill Cody died on January 10, 1917, in Colorado.

play a story that you watch in a theatre

Omaha /ˈəʊməhɑː/

competition a game that people try to win

Annie Oakley

Annie Oakley was born on August 13, 1860, in Ohio. The name her father and mother gave her was **Phoebe** Ann Moses. Her father died when she was five years old.

Annie Oakley

Annie shot animals to eat when she was very young. Then, when she was fifteen, she started shooting in competitions.

Frank Butler worked in a travelling Wild West show. One day Annie shot with him in a competition – and Frank lost!

Annie became Frank's wife on June 22, 1876. She changed her name to Annie Oakley and the two of them travelled round the country shooting in shows and competitions. Frank taught Annie to shoot a ten cent **coin** from his hand.

In 1885 Frank and Annie joined Buffalo Bill's Wild West Show. They stayed with the show for seventeen years. In the show, Annie shot a cigarette from Frank's mouth. She never made a bad shot!

The Sioux Indian chief, Sitting Bull, was in the Show too. He liked Annie and she taught him to write.

The show went to Europe in 1887. Annie and Frank then left Buffalo Bill's Wild West Show to do 'The Oakley and Butler Shooting Show' in Europe's biggest cities. They went back to the USA later.

Phoebe /'fi:bi/

coin metal money

In 1901, Annie got hurt in a train accident. But after some months she was back at work again, this time in a play about her life. In the 1914–18 war, Annie and Frank taught soldiers to shoot.

In 1921, Annie was in a car accident. After this, she and Frank moved to Ohio. She died on November 3, 1926, and Frank died three weeks later.

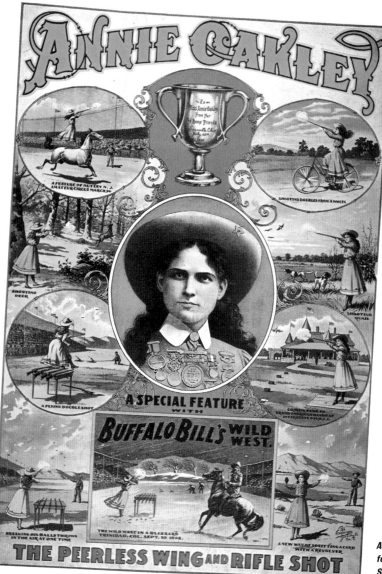

An advertisement for the Wild West Show

Nat Love

Nat Love was born in Tennessee in 1854. Before the Civil War, he was a black **slave**, but after the war, all slaves became free men and women. In 1869, fifteen-year-old Nat left the South to become a cowboy. He went to Dodge City and worked with other black cowboys there.

slave a person who must work for no money

In 1876, Nat helped to take cows from Arizona to the gold-mining town of Deadwood, in Dakota. There, he was the 'best shot' in a shooting competition. After that day, people in the town called him 'Deadwood Dick'.

Later, there were many books about a man called Deadwood Dick, and Nat always said, 'That writer took my name for his stories'.

Nat Love

The End of the Wild West

There is no Wild West today. Some of the stories about the gunfighters and bank robbers of those days are true. Some are not. But they go on exciting us today through books, films, television, and videos.

READING CHECK

Match the first and second parts of these sentences.

a	Kickapoo Indians ...	5	**1**	... killed buffaloes for the railroads.
b	Buffalo Bill ...	☐	**2**	... learned to read with Annie Oakley.
c	Ned Buntline ...	☐	**3**	... learned to shoot when she was a girl.
d	A buffalo hunt ...	☐	**4**	... married Annie after a shooting competition.
e	Annie Oakley ...	☐	**5**	... taught William Cody to shoot and ride.
f	Frank Butler ...	☐	**6**	... was born in Tennessee.
g	Sitting Bull ...	☐	**7**	... was one of the things in Buffalo Bill's Show.
h	November 1926 ...	☐	**8**	... was the name Love got after a shooting competion.
i	Nat Love ...	☐	**9**	... was when Annie and Frank died.
j	Deadwood Dick ...	☐	**10**	... wrote a play about Bill Cody.

WORD WORK

1 Choose the correct words to complete the sentences.

film / play / show

a In 1872 Bill Cody was in a ....play.... about Wild West scouts by writer Ned Buntline.

b Chief Sitting Bull travelled in Buffalo Bill's Wild West .... for a time.

c Gunfight at OK Corral (1957) is a .... about good men fighting for the law.

competition / war / battle

d Annie Oakley met her husband in a shooting ....

e The Sioux Indians killed George Custer at the .... of the Little Big Horn.

f The James brothers robbed banks and trains during the American Civil ....

money / coin / gold

g In the show Annie shot a .... from Frank's hand.

h White men wanted to look for .... in the Black Hills of Dakota.

i Buffalo Bill made lots of .... from shooting buffaloes.

scout / slave / cowboy

j When the Civil War finished, the black .... Nat Love became a free man.

k Kit Carson became a .... for the army because he knew the land well.

l Billy the Kid was a .... before he joined a gang of criminals.

WHAT NEXT?

Here are some more famous Wild West people.
Who would you like to learn about? Why are you interested in them? Tick the boxes.

Davy Crockett ☐
He fought to free Texas from Mexico

Geronimo ☐
The famous Apache Indian Chief

Bella Starr ☐
The first woman horse thief in the US

Charles Russell ☐
He painted great cowboy pictures

Project A

A WILD WEST LIFE

1 Choose a Wild West person from this book. Answer these questions.

   a When and where did he or she live?

   b What did he or she do?

   c Why did you choose him or her?

2 Read about Bella Starr and answer the questions on page 40.

BELLA STARR
(1848-1889)

When Bella was twenty she married James Reed, a criminal. When Reed killed a man, Bella and her baby Pearl went with him to live in California.

Bella had different husbands, and they were all criminals. Her house was a safe place for criminals to go. She was Jesse James's friend.

Bella was bad but interesting. I like her because she was a woman in a world of men.

3 Write about the life of your person.

Project B

A WILD WEST STORY

1 Match the pictures with the sentences.

1

2

3

4

a In the end he gave her a fish to eat and she was happy. ☐

b One day Mary Weston went to the river to wash her dirty clothes. ☐

c She saw the young Indian, Little Owl, fishing in his canoe. ☐

d She felt very frightened. Little Owl was very frightened, too, when he saw her. ☐

2 Write these sentences. Add *a* or *the* where necessary, and put the verbs in the past.

One day young Indian Little Owl *go* to river to fish.

....

He *see* Mary Weston washing her dirty clothes on bank

....

He *feel* very frightened and she *be* frightened too when she *see* him.

....

In end she *give* him cake and he *be* happy

....

3 Look at the pictures on page 44. Tell the story of John Weston and the Indian girl, Running Water. Use these words to help you.

mountains   to hunt   foot   trap

to put (something) on   to take (something) out of   bandage

....
....
....
....
....
....
....
....

John Weston and Running Water

1

2

3

4

5

GRAMMAR

GRAMMAR CHECK

Suffixes: –er

When we add the suffix –er to a verb, we make a word for a person.

Young Wyatt Earp hunted buffaloes. He was a hunter.

When the verb ends in –e, we add –r.

drive – driver   write – writer

When the verb has one syllable and ends with one vowel and one consonant, we double the consonant before adding –er.

rob – robber

Butch Cassidy and the Sundance Kid robbed banks and trains. They were robbers.

In British English, has a double consonant. In American English, the consonant remains single.

travel – traveller (British English)   *travel – traveler* (American English)

1   **Choose the correct verb from the box for each sentence. Then add –r, –rs, –er, or –ers to make nouns, and write the nouns in the spaces. Some verbs may need a double consonant.**

drive	farm	gamble	gunfight	hunt	~~kill~~
lead	love	manage	ride	rob	travel	write

a When Billy the Kid shot his first man, he became a ..Killer.. .

b .... followed the trails to the West.

c The Pony Express had a lot of fast horses and ....

d When Jesse James's gang robbed a train, the .... died.

e Ned Buntline was a .... of Buffalo Bill books.

f In the saloon .... played games for money.

g Jesse James and Butch Cassidy were both .... of gangs.

h Wild Bill Hickok and the .... of the Pony Express office shot Dave McCanles and his friends.

i Etta Place became the Sundance Kid's ....

j Three of the Earp brothers were .... at the OK Corral.

k Frank and Jesse James were the first bank .... in America.

GRAMMAR CHECK

Information questions and question words

We use question words – like who, what, why, where, and when – in information questions. We answer these questions by giving some information.

Where did Annie live? In Ohio.

Question words go at the beginning of the sentence.

When the question word is the object of the question, we use an auxiliary verb before the subject.

Where did Frank Butler work?

After the auxiliary verb or , we use infinitive without .

Where did Annie and Frank take their show?

2 Complete the questions to Annie Oakley using the correct question word: *who, what, why, where,* or *when*. Then match your questions with her answers.

a ..When.. were you born? ☐ 7

b .... was your real name? ☐

c .... did your father die? ☐

d .... did you shoot animals as a young girl? ☐

e .... did Frank work? ☐

f .... did you marry? ☐

g .... did you shoot from Frank's hand? ☐

h .... did you become famous? ☐

i .... did you teach to write? ☐

j .... did Buffalo Bill's Wild West Show go in 1887? ☐

k .... did you and Frank do in the war? ☐

1 To Europe.

2 In a travelling Wild West show.

3 Sitting Bull.

4 Phoebe Ann Moses.

5 Because I never made a bad shot.

6 When I was five years old.

7 In 1860.

8 We taught soldiers to shoot.

9 Frank Butler.

10 A ten cent coin.

11 To eat them.

GRAMMAR CHECK

Possessive adjectives

We use possessive adjectives – **my**, **your**, **his**, **her**, **its**, **our**, **and their** – **to say who someone or something belongs to.**

When Annie was five years old, Annie's father died.

When Annie was five years old, her father died.

3 Complete Wyatt Earp's letter to his mother using the possessive adjectives *my*, *your*, *his*, *her*, *our*, and *their*.

a) .`My`. dear mother,

What a day! b) .... brothers and Doc came to c) .... house last
night. Virgil and Morgan had d) .... guns, but Doc lost e) .... gun
in a fight, so I gave him one of f) .... guns. Then we talked about the Clanton
Gang. They are famous for g) .... gunfights!

The next day we were ready. 'Leave h) .... horses here, boys,' I said. 'We've
got i) .... guns,' they told me. 'Let's go!'

People watched from j) .... windows. The Pony Express manager closed the
doors of k) .... office, and the girl from the saloon put l) .... hands
over m) .... eyes.

Then the gang arrived. They jumped from n) .... horses and shot, but
o) .... guns were faster than the Clantons' guns! Three of p) ....
men are dead now, and so q) .... names are famous in Tombstone. Virgil hurt
r) .... hand, but he's going to be fine. s) .... brothers send

you t) .... love.

u) .... loving son,

Wyatt

GRAMMAR CHECK

Past Simple: negative

To make the Past Simple negative we use did not (didn't) + infinitive without for most verbs.

The Clanton Gang shot Morgan, Virgil, and Doc but they did not die.

The Past Simple negative of is was not (wasn't) / were not (weren't).

Frank James was not the leader of the gang for long.

Some of the stories about Wild Bill Hickok were not true.

4 Some of these sentences are not true. Find them and then make them true by writing the negative form of the verb in the space.

a Sitting Bull taught *did not teach* Annie Oakley to write. ☒

b The US government wanted .... to buy the Black Hills. ☑

c Buffalo Bill gave .... Sitting Bull a beautiful horse. ☐

d Kit Carson became .... marshal at Hays City. ☐

e Nat Love got .... the name 'Deadwood Dick' after a shooting competition in Deadwood. ☐

f Jesse James rode .... 618 kilometres without a stop. ☐

g George Custer died .... near the Washita River. ☐

h Wild Bill Hickok was .... a black slave. ☐

i Frank Butler worked .... with Annie Oakley. ☐

j Butch Cassidy bought .... a bank in Argentina. ☐

k Frank and Jesse James were .... two friends from the same town. ☐

l Sheriff Pat Garrett killed .... John Tunstall. ☐

m Annie Oakley was .... the Sundance Kid's lover. ☐

n In 1879 the Earp brothers went .... to live in Deadwood. ☐

o Allan Pinkerton started .... an office for detectives. ☐

GRAMMAR CHECK

There was and there were

We use there was and there were to talk about things and people in a place in the past. We use there was with a singular noun, and there were with a plural noun.

There was a famous gunfight at the OK Corral.

There were 3,000 Native Americans at the Battle of the Little Big Horn.

The negative forms are there wasn't **and** there weren't.

There wasn't an easy trail across the mountains.

After the battle there weren't any soldiers alive at Little Big Horn.

5 Describe the street in Tombstone on the day of this picture. Write *there was,* *there wasn't, there were,* or *there weren't* in the spaces.

It was a fine day, and a) <u>there were</u> lots of people in the town.

b) .... two horses outside the Pony Express office; c) ....

a rider on the black horse, but d) .... a rider on the white horse. Next

to the office e) .... a saloon, and outside it f) .... two

women in red. g) .... three cowboys at the door of the saloon, and the

women smiled at them.

Outside the jail the sheriff waited. h) .... two guns in his hands,

and i) .... a smile on his face. The deputy sheriff was on a horse in

the middle of the street, and j) .... three criminals behind him.

k) .... any smiles on their faces!

Near the jail l) .... Pinkerton's Detective office, but it was closed, and

m) .... anybody inside it. On the front window n) .... an

open eye, and under the window o) .... two closed eyes. The office cat

slept there in the sun.

49

GRAMMAR CHECK

Possessive 's and s'

We use 's and s' to talk about who things belong to.

With singular nouns we use 's.	*Buffalo Bill – Buffalo Bill's Wild West Show*
With plural nouns we use s'.	*cowboys – the cowboys' horses*
With irregular plural nouns, we use 's.	*mens – the white men's wagons*

6 Match the words with the pictures and write the correct word.

bomb	books	brothers	buffaloes	farm	gold
guns	horse	mines	office	~~skins~~	village

1 _skins_   2 ....   3 ....   4 ....   5 ....

6 ....   7 ....   8 ....   9 ....   10 ....

7 Match the words from Question 6 with the correct people below. Write the correct possessive form in the spaces.

a Native Americans .... ☐

b Ned Buntline .... ☐

c the Cheyenne tribe .... ☐

d a gambler .... ☐

e the white men .... ☐

f the Pinkerton detectives .... ☐

g the mountain men _the mountain men's skins_ ☐ l

h Wyatt Earp .... ☐

i Wild Bill Hickok .... ☐

j Sitting Bull .... ☐

GRAMMAR CHECK

Countable nouns: all, most, many, some, and no

We use all, most, many, some, and no with countable nouns to give
an idea of the number of people or things.

All the Earp brothers lived in Tombstone.

Most of Ned Buntline's books were about the Wild West.

Many of the things in the Wild Bill stories were not true.

Some of the men from the Clanton Gang got away from the gunfight.

Frank James killed no lawmen after 1882.

All
Most
Many
Some

No

8 Write *all, most, many, some,* or *no* in the spaces below.

Think about the famous people in this book. a) ..*All*.. of them were born in the
1800s, but b) .... of them lived to the 1900s. c) .... of them were
men, but d) .... of them were women, like Annie Oakley and Etta Place.

e) .... of the famous names of the Wild West are the names of white people,
but f) .... Native Americans are famous too, like Sitting Bull and Geronimo.

g) .... Native Americans were friends with white men. Sitting Bull was a
friend of Buffalo Bill Cody. But h) .... Native Americans did not like the white
men. i) .... people died in the fighting between Native Americans and the
white men. At Little Big Horn, j) .... Native Americans died, but
k) .... of Custer's soldiers died with their leader.

Once l) .... of the Native Americans lived freely in the Wild West. There
were m) .... mines or cities. Now n) .... Native Americans live on
reservations. o) .... buffaloes live on farms, but there are p) ....
wild buffaloes. And there are q) .... famous cowboys or sheriffs alive today.
Now r) .... the famous people of the Wild West are in books and films.

||| DOMINOES Your Choice |||

Read *Dominoes* for pleasure, or to develop language skills. It's your choice.

Each *Domino* reader includes:
- a good story to enjoy
- integrated activities to develop reading skills and increase vocabulary
- task-based projects – perfect for CEFR portfolios
- contextualized grammar activities

Each *Domino* pack contains a reader, and an excitingly dramatized audio recording of the story

If you liked this *Domino*, read these:

Pollyanna
Eleanor H. Porter

When Pollyanna's father dies, she goes to live with her Aunt, Miss Polly Harrington. Miss Harrington likes doing good, but she doesn't like children very much!

Pollyanna always tries to find the good in everything. She soon makes many different people in her new home feel happier. But is Miss Polly's life going to change for better or worse after her niece arrives? And what happens to Pollyanna when she has a very bad accident?

Five Canterbury Tales
Geoffrey Chaucer

The year is 1386 and the first flowers of spring are here. A number of pilgrims are going to Canterbury to visit the tomb of Saint Thomas Becket, and they all tell stories on the way.

Who should be the stronger in a marriage – the husband or the wife? And what happens when two men fall in love with the same woman? In these five stories from Geoffrey Chaucer's Canterbury Tales we find different answers to these questions from the Knight, the Wife of Bath, the Clerk of Oxford, the Merchant, and the Franklin. This retelling is good for all ages.

	CEFR	Cambridge Exams	IELTS	TOEFL iBT	TOEIC
Level 3	B1	PET	4.0	57-86	550
Level 2	A2–B1	KET-PET	3.0-4.0	–	390
Level 1	A1–A2	YLE Flyers/KET	3.0	–	225
Starter & Quick Starter	A1	YLE Movers	1.0–2.0	–	–

You can find details and a full list of books and teachers' resources on our website:
www.oup.com/elt/gradedreaders